Peace journey

Malak Ramadan

Book	:	Peace journey
author	:	Malak ramadan
Type of book	:	Thoughts
Number of pages	:	70 page
cover	:	Reem hussin
Coordination	:	Maryam Mohamed Sayed
Deposit number	:	
I.S.B.N	:	9782900872291

Nabd Al-Qimma to translate
Egypt - Cairo
Manager: Waleed Atef Hosni
Tel: 01116058384
Mail: nabdalqima@gmail.com

All rights are save©

Peace journey

Malak Ramadan

Dedicated to everyone who seeks peace and to everyone who rejects the noise of the savage world and searches for peace, and your scattered thoughts will meet in this book.

***

I am very grateful to the transient people in our lives who leaves a trail in us ,the divine massages that come to us in our time of weakness to restore strength in us again.

God is for me to tell me that he is always with me.

***

Despite my certain knowledge that I am a great warrior, isuccumbed in the time of my trial. At a time when steadfastness was difficult for my soul ,and I always trust you, o God, because I know that in the end it is good for me.

***

When you see me defeated by the world, don't tell me more advice about my pain ,Ive read so many in books and novels, but give me your hands to lawn on the get my strength back again.

***

When a person gets a blow in their heart, they think that this is definitely their end, but often pain is the reason for building your new personality.

***

The pain will inevitably end, the sun of hope will shine again in our souls, heralding a new beginning in our story because it is not over yet. It d efinitely wont end.

***

Althoug great warrior, Calibri ifaltered in my time of distress. Im still Iraise my head to the sky and ask you ,what are leassons learned this time from this ordeal, ogod and after the passing of day ,weeks and months, imarvel at your greatness and marcy, and my astonishment increases when you descend on my heart with firmness and strength at a time whensteadfastness was difficult for my soul, and ialways trust you because iknow that in the end it is good for me.

***

One day someone told me that iam strong and can bear many shocks greatly, and that this pain did not affect my soul at all, and when I finished speaking, tears fell from my eyes I did not know why!

Is it because every one sees me or because my soul cries out in pain and I don't tell anyone!

Everyone certainly does not see the pain or fractures of the soul within us, nor do they see the impact of the trauma on us. The presence of the Almight is behind me, I ask for help from him, and whenever the world becomes narrow in front of me, I raise my hand and say, o my Lord, I am defeated, so help me, until I win and you see with this steadfastness

***

We could have changed all these Circumstances to stay forever.

***

There is always hope with the spark of hope that tells you that you are here and you will succeed as long as you try. struggle and do not give up, my friend, as long as you are alive.

***

As long as you have gods that rely on him in defeat, know that you have never lost anything.

***

the world is gone, it has become so ugly in my eyes, but will definitely find a happy ending for me.

***

You must respect the law of your grief and give your grief enough time, so that you can come back again.

***

You must realize the miracle of time and
that it is able to heal your soul from the scars
that have been exhausted for years.

***

The time when we try hard to open a closed door in our face and with an added effort, but some times there is another door open for us. If we want to start over, do not look under you feet.

***

What is about him !!

He strengthens my soul and softens my heart, she says.

***

My flowers grow in the saddest parts of you.

***

The more you trust , the more enemies you have.

***

Fuck your depression, fuck your sadness, fuck your laziness, fuck your enemies, fuck you, get up ,this is your time, this is the time for you success, don't waste it.

***

life taught me how to contain my self, my sadness , my break and my peace I learned how to live for my self I have to get some selfishness to love my self.

***

Mental health status; need to look at the sea for hours and stay quiet.

****

The quieter you become the more you can hear .

****

You are killing me, and you are keeping me from dying.

That is love.

***

Yes I am a dreamer. For a dreamer is one who can only find his way by moonlight, and his punishment is that he sees the d awn before the rest of the world.

***

We write so that our throats do not choke with silence.

We resort to writing when everyone leaves us in the middle of the ocean.

Writing is the lifeboat that saves us from the battles of the day.

***

If you been taking it easy when you should have been learning and growing, when you fail you have to live with that. You can talk all you like…but the broof is in the results!!.

***

When it is show time..

Your work will show don't work for the accolades!

Work for the pride

Don't work for recognition…

Work for your pride.

***

To remember…

Your only competition is you.

Where you've been vs where you going!!

Who you were vs who youre going to be!!..

***

Love does not require sex, and if your relationships with one of them are based on sex, run away !!

***

All the painful memories that cut our souls into little pieces that we couldn't put together again, time will restore them for us again so that we can gather our scattering and stand again.

***

My god, I know that you are listening to me now.

All I ask of you is to restore what is inside me so that

I can stand on my feet that were broken by sorrows again.

***

These painful memories will be a funny past one day so wait.

***

No there is something inside my heart that awaits

My soul mate who will bring me back to life again.

***

Not all silence is better than speech, some times speaking with a womb is better than silence.

***

Don't come to me after the day is over, sometimes the long wait kills feelings.

***

Wise king never begin war but prepare for it.

***

God is very, very close, closer than you think and closer to your request that is running through your mind now

That he is close and nothing separates you from him because you are very close .

***

A woman has a huge energy of love, but if she is hurt too much, she is able to turn that love into a hell that surrounds you on all sides.

***

Oh god, I worried too much, and fear lived in my heart for many nights, and my soul passed a lot that I could not bear, and there is a lot that no one knows but you, but I did not trust in your mercy, and why did I trust that one day you will write me a new chance of survival.

****

I will wake up one day reassured, I will tell everyone that now for the first time in years I am calm in the depths of my soul, no more conflicts and no more things that open

My anxious heart I will proudly say that I have passed everything and no one can hurt me anymore.

***

If you are making big enough progress they all be watching untill you get to that point get your head down and work for the love working.

***

Always look for souls who look like you, because next to the people who believe in us, we multiply our capabilities

***

Don't make them steal your calm and then accuse you of madness, but rob them of their madness with your calm.

***

The equation of time is always fair if we can handle it to fix us.

***

Time is not fair enough so must be careful with time and do what we really must do and what we want to do..

***

A place that doesn't give you your value, leave in silence and leave it.

***

When all the doors of mankind ara closed in your face, go to their creator, for he is able to revive you.

***

Good morning

We are still alive, we still have many dreams that

We want to achieve, so do not be sad about what you missed and start again.

***

In human law, you must expect treachery at any moment.

***

There will come a night when your sun

Will shine and you will never darken again..

***

Do not hesitate to say I am sorry at the time of the mistake, as it raises the score of the highest score for the mistake..

***

Attention is the beginning of attachment, jealousy is the beginning of love, friend ship is the beginning of

Sufficiency, neglect is the beginning of betrayal, distance is the beginning of hate, be aware of what is happening around you !!

***

Good morning...

Receive your day with confidence in your ability and work hard no matter how hard the day is, the success is worth the effort.

***

If the whole world is against me, I love a challenge.

***

A terrifying idea to live in this world and leave it without

Anyone remembering you as if you were only a guest of honor.

***

Every year you pass the date of your death

And you don't know it scary !!!

***

Although I am an emotional person, my abilities to let

Go are frighteningly great.

I am able to lift the wrong people out of my life in an

Amazing way if I am hurt by them.

I am not emotionally humiliated but I am more rational .

***

Don't stop until you become proud of yourself.

***

I apologize for leaving you without letting words burn your soul enough I am sorry I left you so kindly! !

I wish you hell forever.

***

you will fully realize the meaning of maturity when you soul burns enough for the absence of someone, and then you will be sure of the truth of your loneliness.

***

When a decision is difficult but it will comfort

Your soul, I fully realize that it is the right one.

***

Never tell anyone about your next plans…

For the massage of god says..

Spend your needs with secrecy, for every costume is an enviable blessing.

***

There is no value in fulfilling a desire that has passed a lot Of time, and there is no value in the arrival of someone After the end of something. what is most important in things is the timing that adds value to things or takes them away.

***

Can we adjust our relationship and get back together!!

***

I always wonder if I can be a light even for one person only, can I guide someone how to shine and never turn off, can I be that dream and that wish!!

***

Don't fall in love with someone who has leftover

Love from their old person.

***

The love of the soul and that heartfelt nourishment

That hurts the most when parting is not the love of from .

****

Containment is comfortable, but it does not revive

Feelings again.

****

The sea tells me that it is a good listener to me

When I let someone down, and I go to him until

I tell him everything inside me.

***

Everyone will leave even if they swear to you all the promises.

***

Nothing compares to a pure world when you are sitting in the rain sipping a cup of your favorite coffee with a brown covered book to tell you and your coffee all the secrets of this scary world.

***

A day will come when your soul will Be relieved of pain, announcing that all pain will Be left behind to make a new beginning without pain and without aches.

***

God knows the breaking of your soul And hears your screams, so he will soon compensate Your heart for all the ruin inside.

***

They lied when they said that leaving will End all problems. There is no word called the departure of those we invented and implemented.

***

I wanted to be the heroine of your story, not to come out of this story with the most severe abuse..!

***

When we repair our relationship with Allah, he repairs everything else for us.

***

I didn't know when I grew up this much I didn't know why all this ruin around me why all this is happening To me now I wish I would wake up from this dream and my mother would tell me not to go to school today because it is raining and prepare me breakfast to play on the computer just that's all I want.

***

You should focus on your current opportunities because the opportunities you don't take advantage of at the time will not come to you again.

***

The decision is your decision to stop the train and get off the train, even if it is not your station.

***

Always remember that we do not forget the memories, but rather we transcend the memories by piling on them the dust of oblivion with memories that are stronger than them.

***

If all the worries of the world are against me and on my back, then in my time of sadness and intensity I can also be a new person.

***

I think the most terrifying thing in this world is that you never know what peoples true intentions are for you.

***

Imagine turning your love for places, favorite food, books and coffee into one person!!

***

Live your life as god has written for you, with the good and the bad in it, with honesty and enjoyment, and when he removes your sadness, learn from him a new lesson.

***

Don't lie in relationships, lying is the worst thing that defiles and ends relationships.

***

Lying is like quicksand, if you like to dive in it, it will swallow you up!!.

***

You must realize that any love relationship is not a sufficient reason to continue the relationship, you must realize that understanding is more important than love, sufficiency is more important than love, love is never a sufficient reason to continue.

***

Balance must be inside any experience we live, our feelings push us to the thing we love strongly, but we must focus well so as not to be the loser always.

***

You must admit that your refusal to accept any problem

In your life makes it grom.

***

Sitting alone is not a sure sign of your lone lines, sometimes it is that you are listening inside your own f fortress.

***

My personal experience with depression taught me things that I didn't know about myself.

***

You cant erase someone from your minds memory, but if you take them out of your heart, that's another story.

***

Choosing your friends carefully means choosing your future professionally.

***

We were not the cause of the pain that happened

To us, but we are responsible for recovering from it.

***

Always remember that after midnight there is another life waiting for us.

***

Don't criticize the one you once loved with your actions, he has a week time.

***

I always told you that sadness does not suit you…so why did you see it befitting me!!.

***

I can be too much of an opportunity for you, but if   I don't see the good in you, I will suddenly walk away from you .

***

There will come a day when dreams that we thought impossible will come true.

***

The only voice I wish to god to last in this life
is my mother voice.

***

This journey begins with patience and ends with paradise.

***

The end…

A letter of thanks to myself telling her that we will overcome everything that hurts us soon.

***